Advance Praise
Powerful Choices, Powerful Life

"Sharon Good's *Powerful Choices, Powerful Life* is a primer for anyone wanting to delve into the topic of making conscious choices. This resource is filled with tools and techniques for recognizing the choices we have, evaluating those choices, and dealing with what might get in the way of us wanting to make them. The Appendix is as rich as the book, containing many worksheets and formulas for making different types of choices. As a Master Certified Coach, I especially appreciated all of the powerful questions included throughout the book that readers can use to assist themselves in making choices."

Leah Grant, ICF Master Certified Coach

"Why is creating so hard? Because creating is the art of making one choice after another — and we get precious little training in how to make strong choices. Life is exactly the same! Sharon Good's *Powerful Choices, Powerful Life* will help you better navigate your creative life and the rest of your life, too. Highly recommended!"

Eric Maisel, *Coaching the Artist Within*

"*Powerful Choices* breaks down the importance of independent decision making and offers the skills to learn how to move forward in life being able to choose your path vs. allowing life to happen. An empowerment is felt when reading this book, an unveiling of confidence. it created a spark in me that allowed me to own my true power and ability to prioritize, clarify, break down and act. I see not only myself, but my clients benefiting from the powerful techniques included in these pages."

Julia Kay, Life and Health Coach, Your Greatest Day, LLC

"Sharon Good has masterfully dissected, and then reconstructed, the concept of choice. She gives us an empowering methodology for making choices and decisions more conscious for reality creation. What a gift!"

Dana Osborn, Deva Inspired Gardening

"What makes *Powerful Choices, Powerful Life* such a valuable asset to your library is the easy manner in which Sharon writes. You feel as if you are participating in a conversation with an old friend. She interweaves anecdotes into the invaluable information and encourages opportunities for the reader to stop and ponder what she has just revealed. Upon completion, you are anxiously looking for the next choice that comes your way. The one choice you should easily make is to read this book."

Laurie Lawson, CEC, PCC, Empowered Life Journeys

"Well written, very practical and filled with clear examples and useful tools, *Powerful Choices, Powerful Life* is a valuable resource for anyone who is interested in improving their decision-making skills. I whole heartedly recommend it!"

Sally Silberman, ACC, BCC
Professional Coach, Mentor Coach, Coach Trainer

"This book is a gem and a 'must-read.' Compelling and concise, *Powerful Choices, Powerful Life* teaches a simple yet potent four-part formula for making great decisions. With this framework, resources and tools, the reader is equipped to take action on what truly matters and make it happen!"

Diana Long, MS, CLC, CPC, BCC, PCC
Business and Life Coach, Facilitator and Speaker

"This book is fantastic. I kept saying to myself, 'yes, yes, yes,' as I would come to different points. The writing is terrific and flows nicely. The journey Sharon takes the reader on is wonderful. And all the suggestions and exercises are great, too. I can already think of someone I'd like to buy this for."

Rob Fortier, Creativity Coach and Writer

"This is an easy-to-use, 'powerful' guide for making big and little choices. As I read it, I wished that I'd had it available many times in the past. The gold star bonus is the worksheets. They're such a great reminder of the previous chapters and a perfect tool for assisting in making my choices. Great job! It's a winner!"

Elizabeth Rudd, Writer

"What a great opportunity to read Sharon's book, *Powerful Choices, Powerful Life*! As I read it, I recognized that she writes in the same clear voice as when she coaches. Through this book, she helps the reader identify the challenge of recognizing the importance of making choice and the power of choice. She then presents options — a choice doesn't have to be just one possibility, but many. And lastly, she presents possible steps that could deeply and powerfully propel the person forward. Sharon's life is about empowering others to be the best they can be, and this is the case with her book — another helpful tool for one to walk toward their destiny, with joy and confidence."

Teresa Craig, Photographer and Writer, Cyprus

"Sharon's words, advice and exercises are an antidote to living a life in the 'default mode', with a busy and cluttered mind. The book instills a sense of calm, clarity and reason to one's personal choices. It inspires me to take control of my life and know I can craft my choices with thoughtful, values-based motivation, which leads to the authentic, one-of-a-kind life I wish to lead."

Deborah Sussex, Creative Nature Coaching

"*Powerful Choices, Powerful Life* is easy to read, comprehensive and life-changing. It will be a real gift for anyone who reads it. Sharon writes beautifully, and I love how she includes personal stories. It was also a great reminder for me that in choice is the power. I can see this as a great resource for my mediation clients."

Tricia Morris, Professional Certified Mediator

"*Powerful Choices, Powerful Life* is one of those rare books that offers up not only an array of wisdom and insights, but also an endless array of practical resources gleaned from Sharon Good's celebrated experiences as a coach. It's one of those reads that will light you up and leave you smarter as you learn all you need to know about how to choose wisely."

Dr. Dominique T. Chlup, Certified Life Coach

"A powerful, clear, concise and practically applicable guide to help you change your relationship with choice completely. You can turn a perceived enemy into a potentially formidable ally and learn to develop an alliance with choice. Here is all the good stuff you were never taught and thus never learned about the power of choice and how to make choice work for you."

Michael C. Dubin, MA, PHR, Living Skills, Inc.

"Ms. Good wrote a comprehensive and insightful book which will surely help many people to understand themselves and their decision-making process. I highly recommend this book to all, including other professionals in the helping professions."

Phyllis Calabrese, LCSW-R

"Sharon Good has written a book on a seemingly simple topic which actually turns out to be incredibly multi-layered, as well as the foundation for everything you want to create in your life. Do yourself a favor — read it."

John Kalinowski, Life & Leadership Coach

"Practical tools for those who feel overwhelmed and perplexed by the decision making process, as well as a great refresher for seasoned coaches and other professionals. Easy to read, understand and apply!"

Theresa Conti, Life Coach and author of *Alphabet Affirmations: Transform Your Life and Love Yourself*

"I truly enjoyed this book and hope many other people will find it useful to become aware of how important even the smallest decisions can be and to start making much more powerful decisions than ever before."

Renate Reimann, PhD, FreshLife Coaching

"Sharon Good's book takes the mystery out of making good life choices. It's a wonderful read with great techniques and stories of people using the techniques to improve their lives. If it goes to series, I want to play the lead!"

Sharon Gless, Emmy and Golden Globe
Award–Winning Actress

Powerful Choices,
Powerful Life

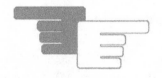

Sharon Good

Good Life Press

New York

Published by:
Good Life Press, a division of Good Life Coaching Inc.
New York, New York
www.goodlifecoaching.com
www.goodlifepress.com

Publishers Cataloging-in-Publication Data

Names: Good, Sharon, 1950- author.
Title: Powerful choices, powerful life / Sharon Good.
Description: New York : Good Life Press, 2019. | Includes 4 charts. | Summary: Provides concepts and examples to help readers understand the importance of making good choices, as well as tools and techniques to enable that.
Identifiers: LCCN 2019901068 | ISBN 9780982317259 (pbk.) | ISBN 9780982317266 (epub)
Subjects: LCSH: Decision making. | Self-actualization (Psychology). | Conduct of life. | BISAC: SELF-HELP / Personal Growth / General. | SELF-HELP / Self-Management / General.
Classification: LCC BF411.G66 2019 (print) | LCC BF411 (ebook) | DDC 153.8--dc23
LC record available at https://lccn.loc.gov/2019901068

ISBN 978-0-9823172-5-9 (paperback)
ISBN 978-0-9823172-6-6 (ePub)
ISBN 978-0-9823172-7-3 (ebook)

Cover design by Justine Elliott

Printed in the United States of America

Contents

You are a decision-making being.

Gary Zukav, *The Seat of the Soul*

Introduction:
Choices and Decision-Making

Decision-making is something we do every minute of every day. Everywhere we turn, we have choices to make, from simple decisions like which route to take to work or what to have for lunch, to life-changing decisions like where to live or what career to pursue. We choose, consciously or unconsciously, our attitudes and beliefs, which have tremendous impact on our lives. And we do all this without being taught how.

Choosing can be a haphazard process, and we may find ourselves clutching for a lifeline when a major decision comes our way and we don't have the tools to make a considered choice. We may think we have too many options or too few, or the ones we have seem equally weighted or confusing. We become overwhelmed and throw up our hands or let someone choose for us. And in doing so, we give away our power.

Living is a constant process of deciding what we are going to do.

Jose Ortega y Gasset

Making choices is a skill and an art, more than an exact science. It's a very individual process, one that's usually developed by trial and error. Having a methodology can be particularly useful when your decision is urgent or life-changing, when you are often thinking the least clearly. By practicing wise decision-making every day, you prepare yourself to grapple with the big decisions in a calmer, less-panicked or haphazard way.

If a particular method is working for you, don't throw it away. Use the concepts and tools offered in this book to expand your resources and open up new possibilities and, in the process, create your own "Toolbox for Choice." As you work with your tools and have some successes, you'll come to trust them more and choose with greater confidence, perhaps daring to take bigger risks.

And there's a bonus: Once you get the hang of it, you'll find your problems clearing up and so many wonderful things happening that you'll want to make active choices all the time!

Just a note . . . some people make a distinction between "choices" and "decisions." Some use one to signify picking from a given number of options and the other as an open-ended selection. You may see a different distinction. If you find making a distinction between the two terms useful, I encourage you to do so. I find it to be more an exercise in semantics with little practical value for me. In this book, I use the terms interchangeably.

SECTION 1

Why Is Choice So Powerful?

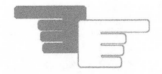

Chapter 1

What Is Choice All About?

"So, what'll it be, chocolate or vanilla?"

"Where do you want to go for college, and what do you want to major in?"

"Where should we go for dinner?"

The questions seem to come at us endlessly. We always have to make up our minds about something. What a pain!

Sometimes, it feels like we're making choices almost from the moment we're born — so much so that we rarely think about them. They seem mundane. If we do it all the time, how important can it be?

It's exactly because we're faced with choices every day — perhaps every moment — that they *are* so powerful. Most of us go through those choices unconsciously, either making them out of habit or by default, not even realizing that a choice was made. We feel stuck in obligations, where we feel we have no choice. Or we give ourselves a narrower range of choices than we truly have. We feel painted into a corner, with little room to maneuver.

By being conscious and proactive with our choices, we can make profound changes in our lives, although sometimes we see it only in retrospect. A seemingly small choice can turn out to be a turning point that has a major impact on your life.

When I was a freshman in college, as a theatre major, I wanted to spend the summer working with a summer stock company to gain experience. I sent out a few applications and was accepted at one company. Because it was a union company, the major roles would be taken by professionals. I would most likely spend the summer backstage doing grunt work and, if I was lucky, perhaps get a walk-on role or two. The prospect didn't excite me very much, but I thought it would be good experience and a good credit for my resume.

I mentioned my ambivalence to a friend, who was also an acting student. She had been accepted to a non-union company, where she would be on stage playing roles in every show. She offered to put me in contact with the director. I called, got an audition, was accepted and chose to spend my summer there. I gained valuable on-stage experience, even playing my first leading role.

But what was life-changing was that I met someone who, several years later, got me into a children's theatre company that I worked with for 13 years. Several of the people I met in that company are still close friends today, all these years later. And what's more, after I had quit show business and started writing, one of those friends, who had also quit theatre and was tryng to establish herself as a writer, became my partner in a book publishing company, which set my life off in other unanticipated directions that are still unfolding.

So, you can see how one small, seemingly minor choice has had repercussions that have lasted throughout my life.

Defining Choice

So, what exactly is choice? Aside from the obvious definition of picking something out of a field of two or more options, choice is the way we make our desires real in the world. Teacher/author Caroline Myss calls choice "the most extraordinary process of creation itself."

To give a simple illustration, say you decide you want a hamburger for dinner. You go to the store, buy some chopped meat, buns and whatever else you use to make burgers. You decide which ingredients to use and mix them with the meat. Your next choice: cook them in a sauté pan, the grill or the barbecue? It's a beautiful day, so you decide to barbecue. You make the burgers and choose between ketchup, mustard or barbecue sauce. And what about side dishes? What should you have to drink? What about dessert? Should you invite someone to join you? You get the picture: The choices go on and on.

In the same way, you choose careers, the people in your life, how you want your home to look, how you'll spend your free time, where to go on vacation and so many other things. It's by making choices that these things become what you want them to be, rather than just passively waiting and seeing what life brings you.

Actively and consciously choosing can make the difference between a life well-lived and one spent cleaning up messes or "putting out fires." I find choice to be critically important in determining our life path. By taking the time to choose, by developing your tools and learning to make smart choices, you'll save yourself a lot of time, energy and emotional pain. That's just good sense. Otherwise, you end up feeling like a helpless victim of life.

One of the joys of being human is that we have been blessed with free will. Choice is how we use our will to bring our thoughts and ideas into form. We manifest our will through intention, choice, commitment and action.

We begin with an **intention** — something we want to have happen. For example: I want to lose 10 pounds.

We then make **choices** to support that intention:

- I will make healthy food choices.
- I will exercise 3 times a week.
- I will get enough sleep so I don't indulge in carbs to stay awake.

The next step is to make a **commitment** to those choices and follow through by putting them into **action**.

While the thought — the intention — can itself cause an energy shift that has an impact on our world, we can reinforce that thought choice with action and commitment. The four together — intention, choices, commitment and action — make a powerful combination. Most of us are looking for ways to lead more fulfilling and joyful lives. One way we can do this is by developing the **skill** and the **art** of making conscious, powerful choices.

But there's a catch: Because we have free will, we can also choose *not* to choose, and this is where we get into trouble. We let other people choose for us, or we take whatever comes — what I call living a "default" life. That would be like getting into a boat and not steering, but instead, letting the current take you wherever it wants to go and hoping you'll get where you want to go. Not very likely. Instead, you'll drift farther and farther away from your target or spend more energy getting back on course.

Choice is a skill, one that, like so many important life skills, we're rarely taught. It comes more easily for some than others, but it's probably because they've taken opportunities to practice. Several years ago, I was editing a parenting book, and the author invited me to take her parenting workshop to better understand the material. One of the techniques she taught was to give children simple choices from an early age. Aside from giving them a sense of control, it gave them a chance to develop this crucial skill in ways that would serve them throughout their lives. This lesson stuck with me, and I've used it in my own life and in coaching others.

Choice is also an art. No matter how skillful you become at making choices, life will always throw you curve balls. There's no way to guarantee that all your choices will work out the way you want. But you can build the "muscle" of choice, give it your best shot, see where it goes and make another choice. As with the sailing analogy, we're always making course corrections, and the more we know about our tools and practice them, the sharper they become and the more accurate our judgment.

Choice requires courage. It's a foray into the unknown, and we need to be able to handle the fear, discomfort and even the sense of loss that accompanies any significant choice. But the alternative is to stay stuck, to drift aimlessly or to not live our lives fully. In looking back on our lives, it's usually not what we did that we regret, but what we didn't do. By developing our choice muscle and making conscious choices, we can minimize the regret we'll feel at the end of our days.

Choice is also a great opportunity. It requires something of us, but it gives back so much more. It's something we can learn, and once we do and develop some proficiency at using it, it can alter our lives profoundly. It is fundamental to who we are as human beings.

So, how can we open our eyes to the choices that are available to us? We can begin by:

- seeing that we do have choices
- knowing the intention behind our choices
- understanding why we avoid making choices

I'll be taking you on a journey to discover how you can use choice more consciously and, as a result, create a more fulfilling life. You'll learn to look at choice with new eyes and acquire some effective tools to help you use choice more powerfully.

So, let's begin!

Chapter 2

Opening Our Eyes To The Choices We Have

One of the core reasons we don't make choices is because we don't know we have them! We fall into habits or limit our thinking based on outmoded beliefs from childhood and beyond. We feel we're "stuck" with our fate, perhaps as a result of choices we made years ago that seem irrevocable or "the hand that life dealt us."

Very often, we have more options than we realize. We may not *like* all those options, but nevertheless, they exist. So, the first step is to open our eyes and expand our awareness to the choices we don't realize we have.

Let's look at some of the ways we limit our choices.

Reasons Why We Feel We Don't Have Choices

∽ **We're taught to follow directions and do what we're told, rather than to think for ourselves.**

When we're children, it's in the best interests of our parents and teachers for us to listen to what we're told. Certainly, they mean to keep us safe and teach us good behavior. But when they're managing two or more kids, they don't always have the time and energy to negotiate everyone's desires, so it's easier to just tell us what to do. They may be so busy that they don't have the time to interact with us and teach us to think for ourselves. Or they may feel that children should just do what they're told and punish us for doing what we feel is right for us. As children, it seems that our very survival depends on obeying our parents' and teachers' rules. Sometimes it does.

Eventually, we grow up and we're faced with more, and more complex, choices ... but we never learned how to make them wisely. We often don't even know what we want. We haven't developed the skills to evaluate choices, and we're afraid of making the wrong one. Or we're afraid of hurting someone with our choices or being rejected because of them. We decide — consciously or unconsciously — that it's easier to let other people keep making the choices and just follow along.

∽ We're caught up in duties and obligations ("shoulds"), both to ourselves and others.

Often, we feel we don't have choices because life doesn't seem to give us any options. We have obligations to our jobs, our families, ourselves, the government, keeping up our lifestyle. And once those are in place, there doesn't seem to be any room for choice without upsetting the entire apple cart.

All of our lives, we have a strong need for approval; it's a basic human need. Different people fulfill that need in different ways — maybe by becoming financially successful or achieving something notable. Others are "people pleasers" who make choices based on what others want for them. They follow the career path that their parents select for them, marry the person who pleases their parents — even have children to meet the expectations of their family and peers.

As teenagers, we're desperate to fit in, and we continue to carry that with us for years to come. Many women feel they have to take care of everyone else before themselves to be loved and accepted. Some of us reach mid-life before we rebel, throw it all away and go live the life we always wanted. But for many, making a drastic change is frightening. Instead, they stay stuck and live lives of quiet desperation.

Making different choices is always possible. It may be scary or challenging, but it can be handled with preparation, integrity, responsibility and kindness.

∽ We've filled our lives up to the brim and feel we have no room to maneuver.

Like our overfilled living spaces, the pace of 21st century living can cause us to clutter our lives. We have jobs, overtime, dating, families, our social activities, the kids' activities, going to the gym, doing volunteer work and a myriad of other things to do. We may have filled our time and our space so full that there's zero wiggle room. You may want a significant other in your life, but have no time to meet someone and no time to spend with them if you did. You may want to add more creativity to your life, but by the end of the day, you're too tired to keep your eyes open.

Before we can add anything to our lives, we may have to unclutter them to give ourselves more room for choice.

∽ We have inadequate reserves and resources.

In order to give yourself breathing room to make choices, you have to have more resources than you need to survive. This includes not only money, but also time, love, support, friends and mental space.

If, for example, an opportunity arises to start your own business, but you don't have enough cash reserves in the bank to support yourself for the six months it will take to get the business on its feet, you may have to sacrifice an exciting opportunity. If you feel the abusive person you're in a relationship with is the only person who will ever love you, or that you can't survive on your own, you may stay in that relationship even though it is physically or emotionally harmful for you. You may have a great idea for a book or a workshop, but you're so mentally exhausted by the end of the day that you can't focus on anything except having dinner and watching TV.

By having a good support system or a reserve of funds, you give yourself the space to take a leap of faith into a new career, relationship or other lifestyle choice.

∽ We just don't see the options we do have.

Often, options exist, but we discount them — either because we don't feel they're possible or because they come with undesirable consequences. One clear example is stop lights. When you come to a red light, you have to stop, right? Wrong. You have a choice. You can choose to go through the red light. Maybe nothing will happen. But there are possible consequences. Perhaps it's 3 in the morning, there are no other cars on the road and no one will see you. But you may also be caught by a policeman or, worse, hit a person or another car that you didn't see coming.

Similarly, you may decide not to show up to your job, but your salary may get docked or you may lose your job. You can choose not to pay your taxes, but you might incur financial penalties or even end up in prison. You can unleash your anger at a loved one, but the relationship may be irreparably damaged; instead, you can choose to handle the situation in a more responsible way.

So, you do have choices, but some of your options may not be desirable.

Conversely, there may be options available that don't seem as possible or doable for you. I can't tell you how many times I've worked with a new coaching client who came to me claiming to be thoroughly confused about what they want to do with their life, only to uncover their passion within 45 minutes. What made the difference was that the coaching conversation turned a remote fantasy into a real possibility. Then, we could talk about how to make it a reality.

When I'm faced with a challenge and I'm brainstorming options, I open the list to include both extremes — the outrageous options that I don't think I have the ability or resources to manifest, as well as the ones I don't like. Generally, the solution falls somewhere between the extremes. By widening the field, you can be creative and open up the range of agreeable options.

✍ **We feel like victims of our circumstances.**

It's a hard truth that we can't control every circumstance in our lives, and things will happen that we don't like and didn't choose. But what we can always choose is our response to the circumstances. We see people who are born with a silver spoon who live miserable lives and people born into impoverished circumstances who live meaningful, productive lives. The difference? They chose how to respond to the circumstances in which they found themselves. Likewise, we can choose at any time to respond differently to the situations in which we find ourselves.

The truth is, we have more choice than ever — maybe even to the point of overwhelm. Most of you reading this book live in countries that offer a wide range of personal freedoms. We can "choose" to use that gift of possibilities to craft fulfilling, powerful lives, or we can go into default mode and give up our power. My hope is that you will take advantage of this book to expand your Toolbox for Choice and that you will use it to create a life more satisfying than you could have imagined.

So, to summarize:

- ✍ We can learn to make powerful and effective choices.

- ✍ We can use powerful choices to manifest our intentions in the world and create lives we enjoy.

- ✍ We can create more freedom by avoiding the problems that occur when we refuse to choose or don't know that we can.

Chapter 3

Understanding Why We Avoid Making Choices

If choice is so important, why do we so often make poor choices or abstain from choosing at all?

This is not meant to cast aspersions on anyone. No one I know ever took a class on how to make good choices (until I started teaching one!). We learn by trial and error, casting around or choosing blindly and hoping our choices will work out.

When we're young, we're often taught to follow directions and do what we're told. As we grow older, unless our parents gave us opportunities to develop some skill with choice, we're faced with increasingly challenging choices and no practice or tools for making those choices. We either take a shot in the dark, hoping we'll hit the target from time to time, or we stick our head in the sand and hope someone will choose for us or that it will miraculously work out for the best. But this often leaves us cleaning up messes or digging ourselves into deeper holes.

Many of us *do* want to make empowered choices, but still we don't. Beyond a lack of skill, the #1 reason we avoid making choices is ... fear.

Fear shows up for each of us in different forms. Here are some of them:

1. We don't want to make a choice unless we can get a guarantee that it will work.

We live in a culture where mistakes and failures are not tolerated well. There are often serious consequence of a bad choice. So, before we choose, we want a guarantee that we're making the right choice. We wait for a sign, which doesn't always come.

For better or worse, life doesn't offer us guarantees. Even the best planned and thought-out choices can go awry. So, we hesitate to choose for fear of making a wrong choice. We think that it's better to make no choice than the wrong one. But by doing so, we keep ourselves motionless, paralyzed. We sit on the fence, praying for a sign from the heavens (or from another person) that will tell us what to do.

When Gail came to me for coaching, she wanted to leave her current career in Human Resources, which had become boring to her, and start a new career in Public Relations. As we began to work on her exit strategy, doubts began to arise, and she thought she might be better off trying for a promotion in her current career, rather than risk moving into something unknown. So, we started to work on that. But then she felt that if her goal was to change careers, she shouldn't waste time on the old one. Again, we turned toward the exit strategy. To make a long story short, Gail went up and back so many times that we finally terminated coaching, because she wasn't getting anywhere.

Newton's first law of motion says that an object at rest tends to stay at rest, while an object in motion will stay in motion at the same speed in the same direction until it's acted upon by an outside force. We call this "inertia." Someone once said to me that it's easier to steer a moving vehicle. If we sit still, inertia sets in, and it takes some outside force to get us moving. If we don't consciously *choose* to move, that outside force is often a crisis. Once you make a choice, you set things in motion. You can always choose a different direction later, but it becomes easier to move ahead once you've gotten things going.

2. We're afraid to make a wrong choice, that there's no going back.

Along with wanting a guarantee, we're afraid that our choice is irrevocable, and we want it to be right the first time. So, we hesitate to commit to a choice until we can be sure it's right. We fear that once we set a course, we can never go back. To some extent, this is true — but again, better to be in motion than standing still. Whatever choice we make will move us forward, and then we can make another choice from where we are.

My client Jake had been laid off from a job as a restaurant manager when we started working together. Jake wanted a change. He wanted a career where he could help people. But initially, it seemed easier to try event planning, which drew on his previous experience. He landed a job, but six months later, he realized he just didn't like the hospitality field and asked for help applying for a social work program. The six months he spent in event planning gave him some valuable information that empowered him to take a bigger leap with more confidence.

Philosophically, we could say that no choice is a wrong choice. Every path takes us on a different route to where we want to go and may offer some interesting lessons and unexpected experiences along the way. By avoiding choice, you're settling for a life that is safe and predictable, but also flat and unexciting. By practicing choice and taking the risk, you learn to make better choices and open yourself up to new and exciting opportunities.

3. We're afraid of the responsibility that comes with stating a choice.

In our world, "responsibility" usually translates as "blame." As children, when we hear, "Who's responsible for this mess?" we know that our parent or teacher is looking for someone to blame and punish. When we hear "responsibility" at work, we know our boss is looking for a scapegoat. We're terrified of making a choice, because we fear that if it goes wrong, we'll be "held responsible" — meaning, "blamed."

Another aspect of responsibility is what will be required of us once we make a choice. We may, for example, make a choice to try a new career or become a parent. Our new choice carries with it new challenges that we're not sure we can live up to. So, making a choice that means added responsibility scares us, and we may avoid making such choices, opting for the safe, but disappointing route.

Actively making a choice means we need to own responsibility for that choice. If we don't choose, we can say it just happened to us and blame circumstances or someone else. If we declare a choice, we have no one to blame but ourselves. And that's a good thing. Taking responsibility is powerful. If you own your choices, then you have the power to change them.

In making choices, we need to deal with the consequences of our choices, build on what we've learned and make further choices. While it may be scary at first, taking responsibility gives us more power and control. Once you see the improvement in your life, you won't want to stop!

4. We feel we don't have the authority.

When we're small, we develop a view of the world that comes from a small, powerless perspective. We depend on those big, powerful people in our life for our safety, well-being and even our survival. We learn to curry their favor and fear their disapproval.

When elephants born in captivity are young and only weigh a few hundred pounds, their keepers restrain them by tying them to a stake in the ground. They learn that they can't break free. But when they're fully grown and weigh six to eight tons, they still think they can't pull free from the stake. In the same way, when we grow up and are big and powerful ourselves, we don't always realize how powerful we really are, and we still fear the disapproval of the authority figures in our lives. We hand over our power so that we can feel safe with them and avoid their criticism or rejection.

If we continue to make choices to win the approval of our parents, bosses, spouses and other authority figures in our lives, we give them our power. As adults, we need to claim that power and authority and learn to deal with conflict and disapproval from that adult perspective. We have the authority, the intellectual capacity and the internal strength to handle these things in a way that we couldn't as small children. While we may need to negotiate a situation with others, we no longer have to ask for permission to be the authorities in our own lives and ask for what we want or need.

5.   We're afraid of the powerful changes choice can bring.

Choice is at the root of change, and change is scary. We may fear that if we make choices, they will change our lives. They will force us to deal with new things, learn new skills and draw on personal resources we've never tapped before and aren't quite sure we can count on. The status quo starts to look really comfortable, even if it's "the devil you know."

We live with the illusion that if we keep our heads down and don't make choices, that change will pass us by. The truth is, we live in an ever-changing world and changes will happen — and they're happening faster than ever — whether we choose or not. By making choices consciously, we can influence the direction those changes take, rather than being swept up in the current.

6.   We feel that we have to explain or justify our choices.

Often, we feel we need to explain our choices to the important people in our lives, and our choices are expected to make sense to them in relation to our history and what they expect of us. If we want to make a radical change, but can't come up with a rational explanation that satisfies other people, we may avoid making that choice.

We live in a world that appears to be linear in its progression. But often, our choices are *not* logical, linear or consistent. We may start down a path, only to find out it's not where we want to go. We may enter law school, only to realize that we hate it and really want to be a musician. Or we may feel called to a life or career direction that is completely antithetical to our family's values.

As a Career Coach, I often assist a client in writing a resume that seems to have a linear progression, so that it's justifiable to a potential employer, when, in fact, my client has been an explorer, trying many different paths. Sadly, some people actually make their career choices so that their resume will "make sense." They rob themselves of the freedom of following their hearts and listening to their inner guidance, cutting themselves off from many exciting possibilities.

In order to make powerful choices, we need to give ourselves permission to weigh both outer and inner voices, and that may mean that some of our choices won't make sense to other people. The heart isn't logical, and it may lead us in directions that are exciting, but unexplainable to others, and maybe even to ourselves.

My client Jeff got his bachelor's degree in psychology, then went to law school to appease his parents. He didn't enjoy his courses, but he buckled down and did well. Once he graduated, he decided it was time for him to pursue his passion to be an actor. His parents weren't happy, but by applying the discipline he learned in law school to something he really loved, he became successful in his chosen career. Ultimately, his parents were proud of him and loved telling their friends when Jeff was appearing in a TV show.

7. We keep ourselves in constant mental and emotional overload.

I don't know anyone these days who doesn't feel that they have more to do than they could possibly handle. Or they're struggling to stay afloat in a world that often doesn't make a lot of sense. We have different aspects of our lives pulling us in a hundred different directions. And sometimes, we purposely keep ourselves occupied with busy work and unnecessary tasks, or we become addicted to our technology, so we don't have to face unpleasant emotions or challenging situations.

In order to make good choices, we need to be able to think and self-reflect. When we're constantly busy, we have no time to sort through our thoughts and feelings. We end up avoiding choice or just picking something to get it over. So, the first choice we need to make is to set aside time on a regular basis where we have nothing to do, no place to be and no obligations to tend to, where we can clear our minds and allow good choices to emerge.

8. We don't know what we want, or we don't believe that what we want is possible.

Let's face it, life is confusing. The world has gotten much more complex than it was even 20 years ago. The good news is that we have many more options than we used to, but that can make choosing more difficult. We may look at all those options, but if we don't have the tools for working with all the possibilities that are open to us and making good choices, we feel totally overwhelmed and shut down.

On the other hand, we also have many old beliefs about what we can do, based on outmoded limitations or assumptions. We may rule out certain choices because of our gender or our age, or we eliminate a possibility because we don't have the skills or knowledge — both of which can be acquired. We may limit ourselves because of beliefs or family roles that were drummed into us as children: "You can't be an artist – you can't even draw a straight line" or "Your sister is the smart one, so you should just learn a trade. You don't have what it takes to make it in college." So, although we may feel drawn to something we want to do, we rule it out because we don't believe it's possible, .

Laura always loved to draw, but when her sister became an artist, she didn't want to compete with her and felt she had to choose something else. Being a photographer still drew on her creative skills, but it was never as fulfilling as painting might have been.

9. We're reluctant to deal with loss.

Very often, when we're faced with making a choice, we're not aware that every choice inherently includes a loss. We avoid making the choice, but we don't know why.

Whenever you're making a choice, you're gaining something, but you're also losing whatever would come with the other options you're *not* choosing, or the life you're leaving behind. So, you need to be aware of what you're giving up by making that choice, and then make room to grieve that.

10. We feel overwhelmed by too many choices or too great a range of choice.

In his book, *The Paradox of Choice: Why More Is Less*, Barry Schwartz talks about how something like buying a pair of jeans, which used to be so simple, has become so complicated, with all the options available. I've had the same experience staring down the cereal aisle in my supermarket. And those are just two examples of all the choices we need to make every day.

By learning a variety of tools for making choices, we can learn to handle the overwhelm and to set criteria that will help us make good choices.

When we become aware of how and why we avoid making choices, we can catch ourselves in the act and make another choice!

As you continue through this book, you'll gain many tools and concepts that will help you overcome your resistance and guide you in making more powerful choices.

Chapter 4

Knowing The Intention
Behind Our Choices

To make smart choices consistently, we need to make them consciously. We can do this by being aware of how we make choices, discerning what works and what doesn't and learning some new tools and concepts.

One of the most powerful ways we can choose is by knowing why we make the choices we do. The more we evaluate our choices, the more powerful they will be. By making choice more conscious, we can mitigate the unconscious forces that influence us.

1. What's motivating your choice?

What's behind the choices you make? Fear or growth? Moving toward something you want or away from something you don't want? Positive or negative intent? Courage or desperation?

Many choices are made to avoid fear and pain, rather than to enable you to grow. A common fear choice is around money. We choose what's safe rather than what our heart desires, because we're afraid to take a financial risk. In some cases, we use money as the excuse when there are other fears that are even harder to face, such as being judged or humiliated, jeopardizing your relationship (which may already be shaky) or pushing yourself out of your safe zone.

In some cases, we make choices as a rebellion against what we don't want. I've seen many people leap into their own business or grab the first master's degree program they lay their eyes on, just to get away from their dreary corporate job, rather than taking the time to figure out what truly inspires them and investing in that.

Others rebel against what some authority figure wants them to do. (Remember the "terrible twos" or your teen years?) But by pushing against someone else, you're as controlled by them as if you did what they wanted. It's important to do the inner work to become an emotional adult and listen to what you truly want, rather than reacting against others. As we evolve, we make mature choices about what we do want and toward what will support us in our growth.

You develop a powerful personal will by making choices that draw on both the desires of the heart and the wisdom of the mind.

Caroline Myss,
Sacred Contracts

Is the intent behind a particular choice to help or to harm yourself or another person? You may be angry at someone and want to get back at them. You may choose something for yourself because you don't feel worthy of more or to punish yourself for something you feel guilty about. A choice like that is a misuse of power, whether it's directed toward yourself or someone else. Again, you need to do the inner work to clear the playing field, so you can make choices that truly serve you.

And finally, are you choosing out of courage or desperation? One common example (about money again): Many people live paycheck-to-paycheck, with nothing to fall back on. When you're desperate, you do what you need to do to survive, even when it makes you miserable. If a golden opportunity comes along, it takes a huge amount of courage to take that leap of faith when you have no way to pay your bills during the transition. And if you have dependents, you can't afford to put their well-being in jeopardy by taking an untenable risk.

It takes courage to make a choice for a greater future rather than just handling the immediate problem, doing what's expedient or doing what outmoded beliefs and attitudes dictate.

2. What are the belief systems behind your choices?

We all have beliefs and attitudes that we've internalized from a young age. We learn or make these up to make sense of the world and stay safe, but they consciously or unconsciously influence our choices well beyond their "use by" date. Belief systems can become so ingrained in us that we don't even see them anymore.

When you evaluate your choices, begin by opening your eyes and looking at what's behind them. If you're not sure what that is, look at the results you're getting and speculate what might be causing those results. Do you have belief systems instilled by your family or others who influenced you growing up that limit your choices? For example, do you have beliefs about what women/men are capable of or allowed to do? Were you always told that you're not good at something that you'd like to try?

My client Fran was considering a career in market research, but she was afraid she didn't have the math skills. I asked her how she did in math in high school, and she told me she got A's! But somehow, she had internalized a belief that she was bad at math. We discussed her getting a math tutor to shore up her confidence in this area if she decided to pursue this career.

Your family or community may have had a belief like: Women who make a lot of money will never find a husband. Down the line, this may cause you to sabotage your career or underachieve. But many men would be thrilled to have two high incomes in the family!

What are your beliefs about yourself? How do you see yourself? Are you avoiding your first choice because you don't think you deserve it or could have it? Have you gotten used to settling? When we fall into this pattern, we may discount certain choices before they even make it to the list because we just don't see them as possibilities for ourselves. For someone else maybe, but not for us. The approach here is to question your belief, to fact-check it and see if it's really true, or perhaps an excuse to avoid doing something you're scared of.

3. How will this choice benefit you? How will it hurt you?

Do a Cost/Benefit analysis. (See Appendix G.) What benefits will this choice give you? What will it cost you? Do the benefits outweigh the cost, or vice versa? Are the benefits good enough to make it worth risking the costs? Is there any way you can enhance the benefits or reduce the costs?

Keep in mind that a particular benefit or cost may outweigh what's on the other list. It's also up to you what your most important values are. My client Alan had a lucrative job in finance, but going into the office every day was literally making him sick. He quit his job to pursue a career in film. His wife, who had "signed on" expecting a certain lifestyle, left him. But Alan realized he couldn't go back to a career that was killing him and made the difficult choice to stay true to himself.

4. Are your choices in line with your values and goals?

Ask yourself these questions:

- What do you hope to get from this choice?
- Does it feel good to you?
- Is there a hidden agenda to hurt someone?
- Are you making a choice that goes against your values?
- Are you making a choice that's easier rather than better?
- What are the likely consequences of your choice in other areas of your life?
- Is this a choice that someone else thinks would be good for you? Do you agree? Really?
- Do you feel like you're selling yourself out in making this choice?

Make sure that the values you adopt are real to you, that they're yours and not someone else's. As children, we take on the values that our parents, teachers, community and religion teach us. As we get older, it's important to question them and re-choose them as our own or come up with new ones that are more authentic for us. For example, your parents may think that medicine is a valued field and target you as the doctor in the family. You may follow through to win their approval, but your heart may not be in it.

Many people who do this end up struggling through a lifelong career that doesn't fit them, or they make a radical change somewhere down the line.

If it's more practical to stay on the path you started on, you can reframe the situation based on your own values, finding your own motivation to stay in the field; or find a way to use your training in a way that feels right to you, such as going into alternative or integrative medicine; or find something completely different that supports your values. Being a martyr doesn't serve anybody.

May your choices reflect your hopes, not your fears.

Nelson Mandela

SECTION 2

So, How Do We Make Powerful Choices?

A Toolbox For Choice

While choice is something we do every day, it's rare that we're actually taught how to do it.

There are many approaches and techniques for choosing. The purpose of this section is to offer you a smorgasbord of tools for making great choices.

Pick and choose the tools that speak to you and experiment with some others.

Never underestimate the power you have to take your life in a new direction.

Germany Kent

Chapter 5

Make Choice Conscious

Becoming a more conscious person is an ongoing pursuit. Learning to choose consciously is a big part of that work.

Very often, we find ourselves in a situation and just react to the stimulus. When we feel threatened, we fight, flee or freeze. We may get angry and lash out, or if we have a different style, internalize it and take it out on ourselves.

The chain of a reaction is ...

Think > Feel > Do

Very often, the thought happens so quickly, we don't see it. Someone says or does something to us, and before we know it, we react emotionally. And then we do something based on our feelings, and the cycle continues. When we're caught up in emotion, we rarely stop to investigate *why* the person said or did what they did.

We can train ourselves to stop in the heat of the reaction and think before we respond automatically. So, we change the chain to:

Think > Feel > Think Consciously > Choose Consciously > Do

When we react, our emotions are, in a sense, choosing for us, rather than choosing with our wisdom. If we can go back and retrieve the underlying thought — to understand what we're reacting to — we can choose to replace it with a different thought — one based on our knowledge and understanding, rather than a gut reaction. Generally, a different emotion will result, but even if it doesn't, we can still choose a different action. Let's look at an example.

Let's say a coworker says to you, "Wow, you look great today." Depending on your history with this person, you can have many different thought responses:

- Does she think that I usually look bad?
- Is he coming on to me?
- What does she want from me?

If you react to those thoughts, your response might be flirty, insulted, hostile, suspicious or many other things, some of which could turn the interaction to an unpleasant one. The other person will react to your reaction, and you can end up in a vicious cycle. If, instead, you take a moment to notice your reaction and think about how you want to respond, you might simply say, "Thank you," maybe smile and move on.

Another way we can be conscious is by seeing how many of our choices are motivated by fear. Generally, it's not one of those grizzly-bear-in-your-face kind of fears, but more the low-grade ones that run through your reality like an underground stream. They're so subtle and ever-present that you don't even notice they're there.

Let's say you're invited to a party and you decline, saying you're busy. The truth is, you hate parties. But if you dig deeper, you may see that you're afraid to meet new people because you're not a very good conversationalist (or at least, you think you're not), and if you meet someone you're attracted to, you'll have to deal with your fears about relationships. So, better to sit home and read a nice, safe book.

But if you look at past instances, you realize that you actually have enjoyed some parties. You'll have friends at this party, they always have great food and music and you do love to dance. So, instead of reacting automatically, you accept the invitation, read up on current events so you can speak intelligently about them and put together an outfit that makes you feel good about yourself.

Sometimes the choice we have to make is painful. It's tempting to just ignore it and let whatever happens happen. Or we're afraid of taking responsibility for our choices; if we don't choose, then we can't be blamed. But the world doesn't stop turning because we go unconscious about our choices. We're still responsible by default. And we still suffer the consequences. So, better to choose your consequences (as best you can) than let them come at you.

Know yourself. Aside from the joy of self-awareness, it will enable you to make choices that support who you are, your values and preferences.

> *Every situation presents us with an opportunity to automatically react or consciously respond: a choice point... We are a product of our choices, not of our circumstances.*
>
> Eric Allenbaugh, *Wake-Up Calls: You Don't Have to Sleepwalk Through Your Life, Love, or Career!*

Chapter 6

Create As Many Options As Possible

A great way to make choice powerful is to give yourself as broad a range of options as you can. Even if your options seem limited, take the time to think out all the possibilities. Sit down by yourself, or better with someone else, and brainstorm as many ideas as you can come up with. Be outrageous. Include ridiculous ideas as well as undesirable ones. The idea is to find as many as you can. Then, play with them. Perhaps a composite of two or more can open possibilities for you that never occurred to you before.

A lot of people hate doing their taxes. They put them off till the last minute or avoid them for years and build up penalities. Instead, you might brainstorm ways of getting them done:

- Get tax software that's easy to use
- Ask my spouse to do them
- Hire an accountant
- Get an extension and take a week off from work to do them
- Quit working so I have no income to declare

Obviously, some of these are silly, but when you feel you have choices, you don't feel so constrained. In this case, you might get the tax software and make a date with your spouse to get them done together.

Having a multitude of options may seem scary or overwhelming, but more options brings greater freedom of choice.

See Appendix A for an exercise on generating options.

Chapter 7

Get The Facts

When faced with a major choice, it's easy to get caught up in the dilemma, blinding ourselves with our limiting beliefs and projections of dire outcomes.

The best way to clear up the haze is to get the facts. When we don't have real information, we make things up or speculate. One of my clients wanted to quit her job and start her own business, but she felt frightened about making a choice that would lead to an uncertain future. We worked on selecting and then exploring some viable options, as well as learning how to start and run a business. Once she had some facts to work with, her decision became easier.

Do some research. Talk to people. Consult the Internet. Check out your data. Get multiple perspectives. Understand that not all information is accurate or objective, and that what's true for one person may not be true for another.

When I started my publishing business, I reached out to other small publishers to network and get advice. One man, who was burned out on it, tried to talk me out of it. I chose to follow my calling. It was a challenging venture, but one that I learned a lot from and that provided many exciting experiences.

And don't get stopped by statistics or dismal media reports. News reports tend to focus on the negative. We rarely hear the positive, good news. Remember that you're not a statistic, but an individual with your own resources and abilities. I've found that when you're committed to an outcome and work toward it relentlessly, you can make almost anything happen.

When we get the facts, we can avoid making choices (or not making them) out of fear and speculation. When working with my career coaching clients, I often see them eliminating a good possibility because of what they think and believe about it, without really knowing. One man wanted to write film scores, but he was a family man who wanted time with his kids, and he thought that career would consume his life. By talking to a working film score composer, he was able to bust the myth he made up and open up an exciting new possibility for himself.

Chapter 8

Play Out Your Choices To See Where They Might Lead

Once you've come up with one or more choices that seem viable, project them into the future. It's like a chess game, where you think ahead as many moves as you can, to see what the ramifications of your current move might be. What is most likely to happen? What are the different possibilities, both positive and negative? What can you do to ensure the positive and prepare for or avoid the negative?

Imagine that you're at a crossroads and each possible choice is a different road. "Walk" down each road. What is most likely to happen if you take that path? Project as far into the future as you can. How does it feel? What is your body telling you? Do you feel excited or do you have a knot in your stomach? With important choices, you might take a day, a week or even longer to imagine you've made that choice, live with it and see how it feels.

Psychologist Gary Klein even suggests conducting a "premortem," imagining scenarios where your choice has gone wrong, then analyze the flaws in the plan so that you can avoid them.

Obviously, we can't predict where life will take us, but by doing this exercise, you may uncover an unpleasant consequence that can be avoided or that may lead you to make a different choice. Or you may see pretty smooth sailing. Either way, you can still fill the gaps in your knowledge by doing the research to gather as much information as possible to make a better-informed choice. Use both the factual and the emotional data you gather.

Be careful of getting into fantasy here. That can be fun and open up new possibilities, but you then need to ground that vision with concrete choices and steps that will get you there, and not on wishful thinking.

Use the worksheet in Appendix B to look at the possible outcomes of your choices.

Chapter 9

Create A Context For Your Choices

We can prepare for making major, as well as minor, choices by preparing the context within which we choose. Start with the big picture and work down to the details. What are the important criteria against which you can measure each choice?

Take the time to decide what your life is about. What are your values? Your goals? Your hopes and dreams? Your vision and purpose? Write them down and revisit them at different stages in your life. If you have a life partner, discuss them together to be sure you're going in the same direction, or at least compatible directions.

Having a context helps you to look at the big picture while you're deciding on a single aspect.

Use the worksheets in Appendices C and D to explore your Values and Big-Picture Goals.

Levels of Choice

There are a lot of different choices that we make during each day, and different choices carry different weight. Deciding what to have for dinner is not as profound a choice as deciding on a career, buying a car, moving to another city or a looking at a health care choice.

While a simple chocolate/vanilla choice doesn't have to be made into a big deal, some other choices can benefit by looking at the layers or levels of choice.

Level 1 — Big Picture Choices

This is a major choice based on long-term values and goals. It may be a lifestyle choice or one based on your religion or spirituality. An example of this might be "to live a life of service to myself and others" or "to make responsible choices and be a good role model for my children."

Level 2 — Supporting Choices

On this level, we make specific choices that support our Big Picture choices. For example, if you choose to live a life of service, your supporting choices might be to have a job that allows you to do volunteer work and to honor your own self-care needs. As a role model, you may choose to honor your marriage, rather than giving in to momentary temptations. You may make a difficult decision to tell the truth about a mistake you made, rather than lying to your children.

Level 3 — Action Choices

Finally, at this level, you choose action steps that will move you toward your goals. To continue with our service example, you may make specific choices about how you do your job — cooperating rather than competing, thinking of everything you do as a form of service, being there to support your boss and coworkers, etc. In serving yourself, you may choose to set aside an hour a day for reading or meditation, learn to say "no" to things you really don't want to do, spend time with people you really enjoy, learn the difference between true service and being a doormat, etc. As a role model, you may choose to honor your commitment to attend your child's school play, rather than being coerced into working late.

Weigh your choices and give them just the amount of energy they merit. When you're clear on your Level 1 choices, your Level 2 choices and Level 3 action steps will come more naturally and will be aligned with your big-picture, long-term goals. If you're clear on what best supports your good health, your menu choices at the restaurant will become obvious, and you won't have to agonize over what to order.

Follow the example on the next page and use the blank chart in Appendix E to work out your own Levels of Choice.

Levels of Choice

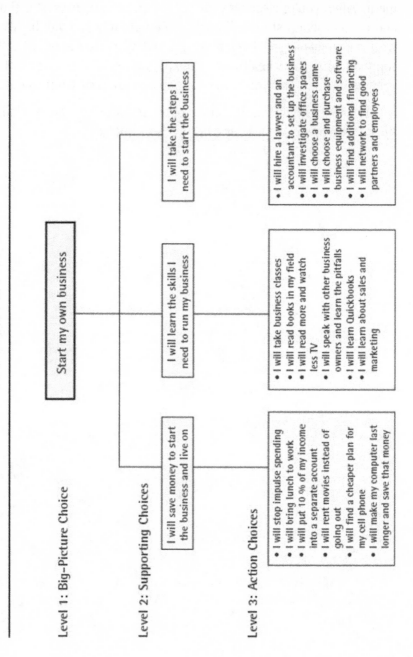

Level 1: Big-Picture Choice

Start my own business

Level 2: Supporting Choices

I will save money to start the business and live on

I will learn the skills I need to run my business

I will take the steps I need to start the business

Level 3: Action Choices

- I will stop impulse spending
- I will bring lunch to work
- I will put 10 % of my income into a separate account
- I will rent movies instead of going out
- I will find a cheaper plan for my cell phone
- I will make my computer last longer and save that money

- I will take business classes
- I will read books in my field
- I will read more and watch less TV
- I will speak with other business owners and learn the pitfalls
- I will learn Quickbooks
- I will learn about sales and marketing

- I will hire a lawyer and an accountant to set up the business
- I will investigate office spaces
- I will choose a business name
- I will choose and purchase business equipment and software
- I will find additional financing
- I will network to find good partners and employees

Chapter 10

Get Perspective On Your Choice

To get different perspectives on your choice, look at it from many different directions.

∞ What is the common wisdom about this choice? Are there statistics or trends? Items in the news?

Remember, this is just one point of view. Statistics can be skewed, and common wisdom changes through the ages. Take the time to dig beneath the surface. Ask, What's really true? Is it always true or sometimes true? Is it true for some types of people or certain circumstances?

∞ What is your gut reaction?

Most of us are intuitive, but we tend to dismiss our gut reaction and defer to logic. Very often, it's the balance of head, heart and gut that leads to the best decisions.

∞ What have you learned from past experience about this choice or similar choices? How might the future be different?

You can learn from the past, but don't get stuck there. How have you evolved? What still holds true? How have circumstances changed since then that could change the outcome of this choice? Will the outcome be better or worse?

∽ What can you expect if you make this choice?

What is the most likely outcome? Where will it lead you? Will it get you where you want to go? What else can you do to make it work?

∽ What do trusted people in your life think of this choice?

Ultimately, you'll make your own choice, but it doesn't hurt to hear from people who know and love you, and whose opinions you trust.

∽ How will this choice affect you, and how will it affect other people?

What will be the impact of making this choice? If you have a family, how will it impact them? Is it positive or negative? Can you live with that outcome, or is it a deal breaker?

∽ How will this choice play out in the short-term and long-term?

Will it solve an immediate problem, but cause further problems in the future? If the long-term results look promising, how will that work for the immediate future? What steps do you need to take to bridge the gap from the immediate to the long-term? If you don't know, how can you find out? (If you can't figure out the entire plan, just start taking steps and figure out the next steps as you go.)

Try these questions on the various choices you're considering. See which one comes out on top.

By exploring different perspectives, you can see both the big picture and the details. It's easy to make a choice based on immediate results or to look only to the future. A wise choice takes both into account.

Chapter 11

Make Choices "In The Moment"

One of the most powerful techniques I've learned is to make choices as they occur. It's easy to go through our day on automatic pilot or defer difficult choices for some future time. Often, we keep ourselves so busy that we can't think straight, so we just do whatever is easiest. Some of those choices are harmless, but others can have negative consequences.

Choices – sometimes even the small ones – are powerful points where we can change the course of our lives and our reality. As we become more proficient at being aware when we're at a choice point, and then choosing consciously, with all our wisdom, knowledge and experience behind us, we can effect incredible change without having to sit down and work at it for hours.

Don't anticipate what is going to happen – participate in what is going to happen! Create your future by being present and actively making decisions in the here and now.

Lissa Coffey

It's also important to stay in the present moment. A lot of the times when we're feeling fearful or anxious, it's because we're projecting some dire outcome that might occur in the future, and then we often ruminate about it. When that happens, stop, bring yourself back to the present and ask yourself, In this moment, am I in danger? (Usually, you're not.) If so, what do I *need* to do to make myself safe? If not, what's the best thing I can do right now? What's my range of options?

Also, don't make choices based solely on the past. History does not have to repeat itself. You change; circumstances change. What strengths or resources do you have now that you didn't have in the past when things didn't go well? What can you do differently to create a better result?

Chapter 12

Look For Choices You've Already Made Without Thinking — Take Responsibility By Owning Them

Throughout our lives, but particularly in early childhood, we make some fundamental choices that we're not aware of, but that rule our lives. Remember the belief systems we talked about in Chapter 4? Like beliefs, unconscious fundamental choices taint the water of our lives and limit our choices. The good news is, by becoming conscious of those beliefs and choices, we can change them.

But, you may ask, if they're not conscious, how do we recognize them? Look at the rules and limitations you've set for yourself. Do any of these look familiar?

- ∽ I'm never going to be as (smart, successful, good-looking) as my father/mother/sister/brother.
- ∽ People can't be trusted.
- ∽ If I want something done right, I have to do it myself.
- ∽ I'm no good with numbers.
- ∽ I have to work harder than everyone else to accomplish the same amount.
- ∽ If I'm honest about my feelings, I won't have any friends.
- ∽ I'm not very attractive.
- ∽ People like me can't _____.
- ∽ No one in my family has ever _____.

When we hold these beliefs up to the light of day, we may find that they don't hold water. When I was younger, I was never praised for my writing, so I assumed I wasn't good at it. When I started my coaching business, I wanted to write a monthly e-newsletter. My early articles were a little sketchy, but with practice, my writing improved and I even went on to write books.

> *Our beliefs create the kind of world we believe in. We project our feelings, thoughts and attitudes onto the world. I can create a different world by changing my belief about the world. Our inner state creates the outer and not vice versa.*
>
> John Bradshaw

Along with those unconscious early childhood choices, we may avoid making choices by letting other people make them for us, directly or indirectly. Maybe our parents decided the day we were born that we would go to law school, and we never questioned it. Or we chose to marry someone in our religion or culture to please our parents and avoid friction in the family, even though we were drawn to someone else. Maybe we didn't realize we had options or we just didn't want to upset everyone by making our own choices. We may not be happy about it, but as adults, we need to claim the power for our own lives and the consequences of our choices, whether we actively chose them or not.

While some of our past choices may leave us feeling imprisoned, we can empower ourselves by acknowledging that we made those choices and then taking responsibility for them. For example, say you married and had a child. Maybe your spouse wanted a child more than you did. You love your family, but there's a part of you that's longing to quit your corporate job and start a bait and tackle shop on the beach. You feel angry at your family for getting in your way, but you would never let them down.

By owning your choices, you can avoid blaming others for them and harboring resentment and act responsibly. Rather than running off and following your dream and letting the chips fall where they may, you can make the most of your current situation, using the time to plan and save for your future. Then, when your child is out of school and your expenses are lower, you can move into your new lifestyle in a more thoughtful way.

It's never too late to take responsibility by accepting the choices you've already made. This may sound like taking the blame, but it's actually a powerful position. If you play the victim, you remain a victim. By taking responsibility, you can start from where you are and create a better future.

Chapter 13

Know That Choosing Takes Courage

It's one thing to talk about making powerful choices; it's another to do it. Some choices will have significant impact on your life, and it can be intimidating to make those choices. By being aware that choosing is a courageous act, you can stay strong when you feel scared or overwhelmed.

You also need to be strong enough to deal with the consequences of your choices. These can be positive as well as negative. A big life choice may shake up your life – your career, your home and many other things. It can impact your relationship with your family or friends. It's not unusual for some friendships to fall away as you grow and evolve. Significant choices will impact your immediate family, so you may get pushback from them as they anticipate the changes it will cause for them. In chapter 4, I mentioned my client who walked away from a career that was making him miserable, only to learn that his wife was leaving him because of it. It took courage to stick with the choice that was true to who he was.

On the other side of the coin, your choices may bring many new successes into your life that will require more of you, that will force you to grow. Facing a scary new level of responsibility may cause you to avoid a challenging choice. By looking ahead, you can take small, consistent steps to prepare yourself for this new phase of your life, rather than feeling like you're leaping off a cliff. On the positive side, facing up to obstacles and challenges is a great way to build your confidence and self-esteem.

We may be afraid of making choices because we fear what might happen. By learning to face and deal with the fear, and to prepare by gathering data and taking baby steps toward our new goal, we become stronger and empower ourselves to make even bigger choices in the future. We can make our lives, and ourselves, what and who we want them to be.

Chapter 14

Know That Every Choice Inherently Includes A Loss

One thing that people often forget is that when you make a change, even a positive one, you're giving up something else. Choosing between two places you'd love to live means giving up the other one. Leaving to start your dream job also means leaving behind cherished friendships with co-workers, who you may lose touch with. You may be excited to have your first child, but there's also the bittersweet feeling of leaving behind your freedom.

When you're not conscious of the loss, you may feel ambivalent about your new choice and not understand why. It may hold you back or diminish your enjoyment of this new phase of your life. As part of your choosing process, you need to allow yourself to acknowledge and grieve your lost possibilities.

Chapter 15

Know That Not Choosing
Is Still A Choice

Sorry, but there's no way out of this. If you don't choose, someone or something will choose for you. Better to have a say in the choice than have it thrust upon you and have to clean up the mess it causes.

A client of mine, who I'll call Jack, shared a past experience that had dire consequences. A friend of his (who we'll call Bob) opened a retail store, and Jack managed and ran the shop. Customers loved Jack, and the store did well. After a year, Bob wanted to sell it and move on to something else. He talked Jack into purchasing the business, even arranging personal loans for him.

At first it went well, but Jack's success as an employee didn't prepare him to handle the responsibilities of being a business owner, and he was justifiably scared. When the bills

If you don't design your own life plan, chances are you'll fall into someone else's plan. And guess what they have planned for you? Not much.

Jim Rohn

came, he couldn't deal with them and shoved them into a drawer and forgot about them. Several months later, he arrived at the store one morning to find that the sheriff had put a lock on his door and shut the business down for nonpayment of taxes. Not only did Jack lose his business, but he still had to pay off the back taxes and personal loans.

So much for not choosing.

One note here: Choosing to *not* act is still a choice. Sometimes, waiting is the wisest course of action, rather than doing something just to get it over with.

Chapter 16

Even If You Seem To Have Only One Option, Or If You Feel It's Been Thrust Upon You, Actively Choose It And Own Your Choice

There are times when it seems you have no choice, or only one acceptable one. If you can't change the situation, what you can change is your attitude. If you go through it kicking and screaming and fighting it, it will be unpleasant and stressful. But if you choose to choose the situation, it gives you more of a sense of power over it.

My client Laurie was informed that she needed to pass a certain licensing exam that was required for her job. If she didn't pass it, she would lose her job, and possibly end her career. The material was dense and boring, and she hated having to give up personal time to study. So, she turned it into a game. She made flash cards of the key material, had her friends quiz her over dinner and rewarded herself after a successful round with a glass of champagne. Once she passed the exam, she treated herself to a luxurious day at the spa.

So, even if your available choices are not pleasant, own them and make the most of the situation. There's power in that.

Chapter 17

Don't Wait Until You're Cornered To Make Choices

When we avoid choice, we wait until we're up against the wall and then make a choice out of fear and panic. Not a powerful way to choose.

Donna was hearing that layoffs were imminent in her company and that she might lose her job of twenty years. The thought of job-hunting terrified her, and she didn't want to deal with it, so she buried herself in work, family and intense workouts at the gym. She figured she'd just deal with it when it happened. When the layoff came, she found that her résumé hadn't been updated in twenty years, her skills were out of date and she didn't have much of a network outside of her company.

Afters six months of unsuccessful job hunting, Donna realized she had to go back to school to gain more marketable skills and actively attend association meetings to make new contacts, and it took her nearly two years to land a new job.

By making choices on an ongoing and consistent basis, you not only develop proficiency with choice, but you can prevent a lot of crises in your life. Certainly, there are things in life that are beyond your control, but choosing to choose affords you some measure of control over what happens to you.

Chapter 18

Choose With Your Head
<u>And</u> Your Heart

Often, in a discussion of choice, the question comes up: Do you choose with your head (logic and reason) or your heart (emotions and intuition)? I say, both. Without emotion, all choices are the same, making it next to impossible to choose. Without reason, you may dive off the deep end into an empty pool. Use both. Find the balance.

In *The Seat of the Soul*, Gary Zukav describes decision-making as "an intuitive process in which you pull data from your mind, your heart and your intuition, relying upon the guidance of your higher self."

We live in a culture where logic and reason are highly valued. But the best choices are made using both head and heart. It's wonderful to be spontaneous, but grounding your impulses in reality can keep you from wasting valuable time and energy going off on wild goose chases. Conversely, making choices only with logic can lead to a dry existence.

Each of us leans one way or the other. If you tend to be logical, check that out first, then check in with your feelings. If you get strong gut reactions, listen to those, and then check out the facts.

In his book, *Emotional Intelligence*, Daniel Goleman discusses how a patient whose emotional center was disconnected was unable to make simple choices, because they all appeared of equal value to him. Values are something we feel, not rationalize.

Ultimately, if your heart isn't in your choice, it's going to be hard to force yourself to follow through.

One last note on this: Be careful of "shoulds." When you do what you think you *should* do, you're not paying attention to your head *or* your heart. Make sure you check in with both, rather than blindly following a "should."

Chapter 19

Take Your Time

If possible, don't rush into a major choice. Take the time to do your research and contemplate your options. Many times, the best choice will emerge naturally if you give it time.

Don't necessarily take the first option that occurs to you (unless you're clear on it or it's a simple vanilla/chocolate choice). Your habitual first response may be one that comes from fear or insecurity. Stop the knee-jerk reaction and think through your options.

Do you homework, then put it aside. Often, when your choices seem confusing, by letting them rest for a day or more, clarity emerges. Think about something else. Do something fun and relaxing. Then, come back to it with renewed perspective.

> All of the researchers agree we make associations that lead to creative ideas when we drift away from the linear, well-practiced solutions and let our thoughts wander, even to ideas that seem silly and far-fetched. "It's when we let our brain flit from one thought to the next — generating images, voices, thoughts, and feelings — that we come up with creative solutions," Mason says.
>
> "Daydreaming Redefined" by Sheryl Seyfert, interviewing psychologist Malia Mason; *Creative Living* magazine, Spring 2009

Chapter 20

Learn To Prioritize

Prioritizing is another type of choosing. People are so stressed these days because they give everything in their life equal weight, and they run themselves ragged trying to do it all. There are times when you have to choose where you will spend your precious time and energy.

You may be faced with an array of things you need and want to do, and you don't know where to begin. In *The 7 Habits of Highly Effective People**, Stephen Covey points out that we tend to give priority to what's urgent rather than what's important**. While the urgencies need to be taken care of, we also need to make time for the things that are important to us — the dreams and goals we want to achieve that don't have deadlines — rather than continuously putting out fires.

Prioritizing can be about big life choices — making a career change, moving to a new location, committing to a life partner — as well as the small daily choices. There's nothing wrong with surfing the Internet, browsing your social media accounts or playing computer games, but you might want to get to the gym or study for your final exam *before* you do that.

*Habit 3: Put First Things First
**Google "Stephen Covey Time Management Matrix" for examples.

There's a wise old saying: Work first, play later. When you give priority to the important things in your life, you can then fit in less important things without guilt.

See Appendix F for a grid that you can use to prioritize your options, Appendix G to do a Cost/Benefit or Benefit/Risk Analysis, and Appendix H for an exercise on staying true to your objective.

> *Sometimes the best way to discover what really matters is to release what doesn't, and see what's left behind.*
>
> Cheryl Richardson, *Waking Up in Winter*

Chapter 21

Commit To Your Choices

It's tempting to sit on the fence and never actually choose, to always be in the process. But that's the same as not choosing. It keeps you stuck.

If you were trying to break a board, what do you think would be more effective: patting it tentatively or giving it a good, strong karate chop? It's the same with life. If you hold back, you'll get tepid results. If you give it your all, you're more likely to succeed. Sure, you can make a mistake. But then you get to learn from your mistake and choose again. If a horse never leaves the gate, its chances of winning the race are nil. By trying and giving it your all, you learn what you need to do better the next time. Nobody makes it to the Olympics by running the course just once.

This powerful quote speaks for itself:

> "Until one is committed, there is hesitancy, the chance to draw back, always ineffectiveness. Concerning all acts of initiative (and creation), there is one elementary truth, the ignorance of which kills countless ideas and splendid plans: that the moment one definitely commits oneself, then Providence moves too. All sorts of things occur to help one that would never otherwise have occurred. A whole stream of events issues from the

decision, raising in one's favor all manner of unforeseen incidents and meetings and material assistance, which no man could have dreamed would have come his way.

"I have learned a deep respect for one of Goethe's couplets:

"'Whatever you can do, or dream you can, begin it!
Boldness has genius, magic, and power in it.'"

W.H. Murray, from The Scottish
Himalayan Expedition

Make the commitment and let the universe support you in unexpected ways!

Chapter 22

Take Action On Your Choices

Choosing itself is a powerful action, but you need to take those choices into the physical world through action. Otherwise, you're living "in potentia."

It's easy to decide that you want to be or do something and then spend hours fantasizing about how great it's going to be and how great you're going to be. Taking action forces you to face the reality. Sure, you may not win the Academy Award on your first acting job – or ever – but when you're actually doing it, it increases the probability that you'll be successful at it.

Janis loved writing since she was a child. She dreamed of writing the "Great American Novel" and fantasized about being a best-selling author, but she was so scared of failing that she never even started writing. We worked on getting her past the fear by starting with realistic baby steps. She got a book of writing prompts and did one a week for 3 months. She started to like what she was writing. From there, she moved to short stories and eventually started writing her first novel. She was so proud of it that she decided to self-publish to get it "out there," while she continued writing and building up a body of work to approach agents.

Facing your fears can be scary, but having small successes is a lot more fun than fantasizing about big ones. And small successes can lead to bigger ones. You may never be the "big fish" you fantasized about, but a small, real success certainly outweighs an imagined big one.

Sure, you might make a risky choice. But moving forward is better than standing still, and once you're moving, it's easier to course correct by making a better choice based on what you've learned. And the only way you can know if something will work is by stepping into it.

So, once you've chosen what to do, make the choice to actually do it. Start with baby steps, enjoy each little success, deal with the disappointments and go for it, or chalk it up to experience and choose something else.

Chapter 23

Know When To Lighten Up

Not every choice is life and death. It's important to distinguish between the life-changing choices, the turning point ones and the trivial ones and give the proper weight to each one. When we fret about everything, we drain our precious energy and make things harder for ourselves. Deciding which restaurant to take your spouse to for your anniversary may be meaningful, but it's probably not life-changing or even a turning point.

Very often, we make mountains out of molehills by worrying about all sorts of things, but we never stop to think whether there's really something to worry about. It's important to consider the real-life impact of your choices and let go of worrying about the unimportant ones.

Linda had been through a difficult divorce and was still weighed down with processing her feelings. She woke up stressed every day, struggled getting out of the house and was worried that she was always half an hour late to work. I asked her what the consequences were for being late and she said, "Nothing, really." I suggested that for one week, she take the pressure off and get to work whenever she got there. That week, she was on time every day!

As they say, don't sweat the small stuff.

We live our lives as if they were one big emergency! We often rush around looking busy, trying to solve problems, but in reality, we are often compounding them.

The first step in becoming a more peaceful person is to have the humility to admit that, in most cases, you're creating your own emergencies. Life will usually go on if things don't go according to plan.

Richard Carlson

Chapter 24

Practice, Practice, Practice!

Choice is a skill, not a talent. The more you practice it, the better you'll get at it. Learn from your mistakes, so that you can make better choices the next time. Forgive yourself for making a "mistake" — all choices lead you to the next choice and the next chance. Choose to learn from the outcomes of every choice you make.

Become aware of the choices you make every day, even the inconsequential ones. Should I brush my teeth in the morning, the evening or both? What should I wear today? If I watch the news for five more minutes, will I miss my train? Do I want decaf or regular coffee this morning? Should I have my coffee before or after I check in with my boss? Should I have lunch delivered or go out? Should I take my umbrella? And so on.

Most of these choices take very little thought. But by becoming aware of the choice process, you become more conscious and proactive. This might not mean much when it comes to these minor decisions, but building this "muscle" will serve you well when a major decision comes along.

As you practice the techniques in this book, notice which ones work for you and which don't. Try different approaches and fine-tune your choice strategy.

SECTION 3

What Else Should I Know About Choice?

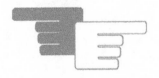

Chapter 25

Choice And Other People

We don't make choices in a vacuum. Our choices may impact others, and others may impact our choices. We live in a family, a work environment, a culture, and each of these has certain values and preferences. We want to fit in, to make others happy, to get approval, to not make waves. This is going to influence our choices.

Author Caroline Myss talks about detaching from our "tribe." If we are to truly individuate, there comes a time when we need to rebel against the cultural status quo and find our own way. Your tribe is not going to be happy about this. They may feel threatened, angry or concerned for your well-being. Ultimately, we may choose some of the same things our tribe taught us, but they will be our own choice, not a given.

It comes down to balance. You don't want to be such a maverick that you alienate everyone, lose your family and your job. But you don't want to completely give your power over to them either. With a little finessing, you can find the balance and make appropriate compromises that don't threaten your values. By using communication and creativity, you can often come up with choices that work for your individual self and include the tribe. You can maintain your individuality, while being a part of the tribe.

Ultimately, if the choices you're making to appease your tribe are making you sick or depressed, you need to make your self-care a priority. I can't tell you how many times I've heard of people who left a job that was making them sick and miserable, and once they got out of the toxic situation, their health improved.

As always, handle your choices responsibly, but make choices that support your health and well-being, even if it upsets others. Women in particular tend to put themselves last and make choices that benefit everyone but themselves. It's like the old adage: If you don't put your oxygen mask on first, you won't be any good to anyone else.

Many of us are afraid of taking the steering wheel in our lives. We're afraid of being left alone with only ourselves to depend on. If you've been giving away your power for a long time, when you begin to take it back, the people in your life are not going to take it quietly.

The danger here is getting into power struggles. If you're a gentle person who hates conflict and you're up against someone loud or forceful, it will be tempting to back down and let them have their way. You may need to take a course or work with a therapist to learn to speak up for your needs. You might end up leaving a relationship with someone who's bullying you or a debilitating work situation. As you become stronger and make different choices, you may lose some people in your life, but there are plenty of others out there who will appreciate you for your authentic self.

When other people are affected by your choices, you may decide out of guilt. You may sacrifice yourself to please someone else at your expense. While there are times when this is appropriate, such as a parent doing something loving for the good of their child, doing it out of guilt doesn't serve anyone. Your choice may force someone to face a choice that they're afraid of, but I've learned from experience that when you make a choice that honors your values and integrity, it will "shake out" for the best for everyone in the end.

Carol and her mother, Doris, had a codependent relationship. Doris felt more in control when she controlled Carol. But Carol felt trapped and resentful. As she grew stronger, she asserted her independence more. Doris didn't like it, but ultimately, it forced her to develop more of her own friendships, and she enjoyed taking classes and traveling with her new friends.

While choice may seem a burden at times, it's one of our greatest human gifts. If you don't choose, there's always somebody who would be happy to do it for you. It may seem that this is keeping you safe and absolving you from responsibility, but it costs you your freedom, autonomy and power. Many women have handed their power of choice over to their husbands, only to be knocked for a loop when the marriage ended and they had no experience making their own choices. Even children need to be taught to make their own choices, so they move into adulthood prepared to do so.

Chapter 26

What About Intuition?

While I'm not an expert in intuitive development, I do know that it's a powerful component of choice. Intuition is something you can develop — it's a skill, just like choice — and there are books and classes to help you. The more you use it, the more reliable it will become; you'll also come to know when it's not your intuition speaking, but your fear.

Most people experience their intuitive "hits" in their body, or they get a strong emotional feeling about something. If you feel so inclined, you can also develop a rapport with such tools as the I Ching, tarot cards, pendulums and other divination tools. Even if you utilize these tools, in the end, always trust your own instinct and reason. If the direction suggested by the tool doesn't feel good and promises negative consequences,

Our insistence on valuing science over intuition ignores findings that when we combine the two, we often make better decisions.

Alberto Villoldo, PhD

don't do it, no matter what the cards say. If you choose to consult a professional reader, the final choice is still yours. While some are very accurate and trustworthy, even the best have been known to be wrong, and you should never give your power away to them. Use them as a guide, not an authority.

If you do want to develop your intuitive power, start with small, low-risk choices and work your way up to more consequential ones as you gain trust and competence. Use intuition and divination tools as part of your information gathering, but don't limit yourself. Use all the input that's available to you on all levels.

For some people, prayer is part of their decision-making process. You may say a prayer requesting a dream that will give you additional insight, or you may ask that your choice be blessed by your higher power. If this feels good to you, add it to your Toolbox for Choice.

No matter how logical or illogical you are about making choices, there are times when miracles just happen. I've worked with clients who have taken logical steps in pursuit of answers, and sometimes the solution comes "out of left field," and it's better than anything they could have imagined.

When Celine came to me to find a new career direction, she was still recovering from a serious health issue that limited her energy. She wanted to work, but she could only handle part-time hours. As her coach, I was concerned that her options would be limited. I had to trust that the right thing would show up.

As Celine started exploring some of the possibilities that came up during the career exploration process, she interviewed a professor in the field that most appealed to her. Amazingly, he happened to be looking for a part-time assistant. They got along really well, he was willing to work with her limitations, and he hired her on the spot.

So, even if you're someone who likes to weigh the data when making decisions, don't rule out those intuitive nudges you may experience.

Chapter 27

Can You Make Bad Choices?

This is a question that comes up often, and there's no pat answer. Certainly, some choices will have more positive outcomes than others, and some have serious consequences. But choices are not always clear. Sometimes, you have to make a choice between the lesser of two evils, or you may want to choose something that's very positive for you, but hurts someone you love. Choices can be tough. And you never know how they're going to turn out.

When actor Tony Shalhoub was young, he had just finished a Broadway play and was offered a role in another play. He felt it was time for him to go to Los Angeles, so he turned it down. The actor who took the part won a Tony Award, while Tony was struggling in LA. But if Tony hadn't gone to LA, he wouldn't have met the love of his life, and within 2 years, his career went on an upward trajectory that led to his breakout TV role as *Monk*, numerous awards and many more outstanding roles..

Some say that there are no bad choices, that every choice is an opportunity to learn and make a course correction. My feeling is that a bad choice is one that we don't learn from and continue instead to make the same destructive choices.

Inevitably, you will make some bad choices. Even if you've thought it through thoroughly, you can't predict what will happen. There are two things you can do: take responsibility and then make another choice. If your choice causes damage to yourself or someone else, do as much damage control as you can. Make apologies, repair the damage, pay the consequences. Then, use the new information you've acquired as a result of that choice to make a new and better one.

The best you can do is make your choices as consciously as possible. Consult with your head, heart *and* gut. Use the tools in this book. Learn to see all the options you have, to look at all the aspects of your choices, and to evaluate those choices to make the best ones. It takes practice, and you'll get better the more you actively choose.

We're always facing new choice points. In some cases, if the choice you made is not going well, you can backtrack and make a different choice. If that's not possible, assess the situation from where you are and make the next best choice.

There's no way we can control the outcome of every choice we make; there are too many unknowns. But what we can control is how we respond to what life throws at us, re-evaluate and make better choices going forward. A bad choice would be to feel sorry for ourselves, look for someone to blame, and perhaps abstain from making any further choices. The only way we can improve our choice-making is to analyze what went wrong, how we would have done it in retrospect, and let our next choices stand on the shoulders of experience.

> *"There really is nothing to lose, only something to gain, whatever the choices you make or actions you take in life. . . . You can actually shift your thinking in such a way as to make a wrong decision or mistake an impossibility."*
>
> Susan Jeffers, *Feel the Fear and Do It Anyway*

Chapter 28

What Happens Once You've Chosen?

Once you've chosen, get behind your choice and do what you can to make it work. Second-guessing yourself drains your energy and focus. There's a saying, It's not about making the right choice, it's about making a choice and making it right. Dive into it 100%. When you're fully committed to your choice, it's more likely to work out well.

Do the practical work. Create a plan. Work backwards from your desired outcome and break it down into specific steps. When you know what needs to be done and have a clear path, you're more likely to take those steps.

In making your plan, if you've seen any potential obstacles, what can you do to avoid or mitigate them? What kind of help or support do you need to bolster your chances of success? If unanticipated opportunities come up or something changes, rework your plan so it stays current. (See chapter 8 for more on playing out your choices.)

In some cases, you may make a choice, but not have a clear idea how you're going to get there. Take it a step at a time and learn as you go. I liken it to walking through fog. Even if you can only see 2 steps in front of you, when you take one step, that opens one more step to you. Often, when you commit to a path, people and things will show up to help you that you couldn't have planned or predicted if you stayed sitting on the sidelines.

If the choice doesn't work out, then make another choice based on the new information you have now. Don't waste time and energy looking for someone to blame. Taking responsibility for your choices also means that you're the one who has the power to change them.

The opportunity to choose never ends. Every choice will lead to more choices. As you build your choice "muscle," you'll become more proficient at facing these choices — the easy ones and the difficult ones — and making better choices each time.

Chapter 29

What About When Stuff Just Happens To You?

No matter how much you try, you can't control everything in life. But you can choose how to respond.

Every moment is a new choice point. If life throws you a curve ball, you may have to throw away everything and start fresh from this new vantage point.

The trick is to have a well-thought-out plan, but not be so rigid about it that you have no wiggle room to make adjustments when more information becomes available. Anticipate whatever bumps in the road you can and prepare yourself as well as you can. Then, put yourself in "drive" mode and go for it!

Chapter 30

And Finally ...

We've covered a lot of ground. Hopefully, you now feel more empowered to take charge and make powerful choices, so that you can experience a powerful life.

A few key points we've covered:

- ∽ Choice is a skill that you can learn and practice.
- ∽ Start with small, inconsequential choices and work your way up.
- ∽ Be conscious as you make decisions throughout the day.
- ∽ Know your values and what you want, so you have a context for making choices.
- ∽ Understand that choosing takes courage.
- ∽ Whether you're happy with your choices or not, you can always make another one. The point of power is Now.

It doesn't matter what choices you made in the past. It's always a new moment. By making powerful choices, you can change your reality, and your future, at any point.

One thing that Oprah knows for sure is "that I created this happiness by choice. And I know it's really not just one choice that matters — it's all the baby choices that will lead you to the ultimate moment, when you can make the strongest stand and commitment to yourself and the life that's calling your name."

APPENDICES

Tools and Resources

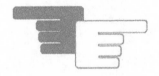

Appendix A: Generating Options

The rationale behind this exercise is that the more options you have for any given choice, the greater your freedom to choose. If you have one option, you're limited to doing it or not. But if you have numerous options, you can pick one or creatively mix and match pieces to come up with your optimal choice.

The point of Generating Options is to come up with as many choices, or options, as you can. Choice is power, and the wider your range of choices, the greater your ability to come up with a powerful one.

Begin by stating the decision you need to make:

List as many options as possible, even if they're undesirable or seem far-fetched or impossible.
Be imaginative. Be practical. Be ridiculous. If possible, include one or more additional, preferably unbiased, people in the brainstorming process to help you expand your thinking.

From your list, choose or distill 3–5 reasonably realistic possibilities. Some of these may be combinations or modifications of some of the items on your list. Choose options that feel positive (or at least less negative), achievable and realistic for you.

To make your final choice, ask yourself the following questions about each of your possible options:

- Is this something I can see happening? If not, how would I need to change or grow, or what would I need to do, to make this a real possibility for me?
- Are there actions I can take that will lead me to this goal?
- What are the potential benefits of this choice?
- What are the possible negative consequences of this choice?
- How will this choice impact me?
- How will this choice impact any other people involved?

Appendix B: Playing Out Your Choices

Complete this worksheet for each of the options you're considering, then compare the various options. If you need more space, use your own notebook or digital file.

State or describe this option.

Projecting forward, what do you think is the likely outcome of this option?

What are the positive points? What will you gain?

What are the negative points? What will you lose?

Of the negative points, is there any that would be a "deal-breaker" (i.e., that you would be absolutely unwilling to have happen)?

How do you feel when you think about this option?

Who else will be impacted by this choice? How will they respond to this option? Is that a valid response, or is it something you need to be prepared to manage?

Is there anything that you're avoiding looking at about this option?

Repeat this exercise for each of your options and see how they compare.

Appendix C: Values

Values provide the compass for the decision-making process. When you're clear what your values are, you can hold your choices up against the background of your values and see how they fit.

What are the values and principles that are important to you?

Who are the people who are important in your life?

What people/things/principles *must* you have in your life – the non-negotiables?

What else is important to you?

Prioritize your list of values, listing the most important ones first.

As you think about the choice you're facing, how do the options stack up against your important values?

Appendix D: Big-Picture Goals

Rather than making choices based on minutiae, let's look at the big picture of your life and *then* work down to the details.. Once you're clear on the big stuff, the smaller decisions will fall easily into place. If your current priority is to work part-time so you can be home for your kids, when a great job offer comes along and it's full-time and involves a 2-hour commute, your decision will be clear.

What are your goals for your personal life?

What are your goals for your professional life?

What is your 1-year plan?

Your 5-year plan?

Your 10-year plan?

Your 20-year plan?

What do you want to leave as your legacy? What do you want to be known for?

Appendix E: Levels of Choice

See chapter 9 for an example of how to use this chart.

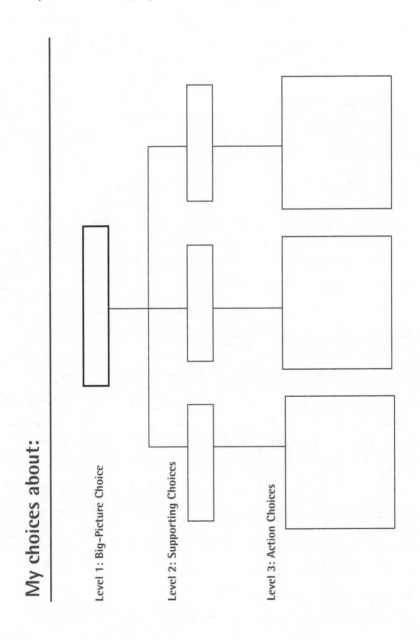

My choices about:

Level 1: Big-Picture Choice

Level 2: Supporting Choices

Level 3: Action Choices

Appendix F: Prioritizing Grid

Begin by listing your options. In this case, we're working with the top 5 options, but you're not limited to that number. For example:

1. Go back to school for an MBA to advance my current career

2. Start my own business

3. Buy a franchise

4. Change careers

5. Look for a new job in the same industry

In the grid, write each option, or a representative word or two, across the top row and down the left column. In the grid, compare each pair of options. Write your preference of the two in the box. (Note that you'll be comparing each pair twice. If you're on the fence, it may go one way one time and the other way the next time.)

	Option 1: MBA	Option 2: Own business	Option 3: Franchise	Option 4: New career	Option 5: New job
Option 1: MBA		Own business	MBA	MBA	New job
Option 2: Own business	Own business		Own business	MBA	New job
Option 3: Franchise	MBA	Own business		New career	New job
Option 4: New career	MBA	Own business	Franchise		New job
Option 5: New job	New job	New job	New job	New job	

Finally, count up the number of times each appears:

Option 1 (MBA): _5_ Option 2 (Own business): _5_ Option 3 (Franchise): _1_ Option 4 (New career): _1_ Option 5 (New job): _8_

Here, it becomes clear that this person would prefer a new job to the other options available. They would then look at the practical implications.

Use the worksheet below to do your own. You can create a larger grid, using paper or a Word or Excel file, to accommodate more options.

My five options:

Option 1. _____

Option 2. _____

Option 3. _____

Option 4. _____

Option 5. _____

	Option 1:	Option 2:	Option 3:	Option 4:	Option 5:
Option 1:					
Option 2:					
Option 3:					
Option 4:					
Option 5:					

Count up the number of times each appears:

Option 1: ____ Option 2: ____ Option 3: ____ Option 4: ____
Option 5: ____

Outcome or insights:

Appendix G: Cost/Benefit Or Benefit/Risk Analysis

This is another great decision-making tool, a variation on the Pros and Cons list. You can use it to evaluate a particular aspect of your life or to compare two possibilities.

Let's say you're not happy in your job, but you feel uncertain about leaving it. A Cost/Benefit analysis can help you evaluate what you're gaining or losing for each option, as well as the benefits and risks involved. Here's how it might look:

Option 1: Staying in your current job

BENEFIT	COST
Decent salary	Dread going into work
They know me, so I don't have to prove myself	Don't feel I'm fulfilling my potential
Don't have to deal with interviews	Bored
Good benefits: health insurance, profit-sharing, etc.	Possibility of making more money elsewhere
I know the work and it's easy	Exhausted at the end of the day/week
It's comfortable and familiar	

Option 2: Looking for a new job

BENEFIT	RISK
New possibilities	Might not like the new job
Could be more interesting or even exciting	Might not get along with boss and coworkers
Might make more money	Might make less money
Learn new skills	Too old to make a big change
Meet new people	Have to learn new skills I might not be good at
	Job hunting is a pain in the a**

Now, you try it! Use the Cost/Benefit and Benefit/Risk worksheets on the following pages to evaluate your options.

OPTION: _____

BENEFIT	COST

OPTION: _____

BENEFIT	RISK

Appendix H: Staying True To Your Objective

As you make choices along the way, keep your overall objective in mind.

∾ What is your objective?

∾ What values support this objective?

∾ What choice are you facing in this moment?

∾ Looking at the different options, which one(s) best support your overall objective?

Here's an example:

Objective: Downsize by moving to a smaller home and selling the vacation cottage.

Values: Now that the kids are grown, we have the freedom to travel more. The vacation cottage was great for family vacations, but now my husband and I want to see more of the world while our energy is good. By downsizing, we'll have less responsibility and more money to fund the big trips we've been dreaming of for the last 30 years.

We also want to continue living in an attractive and safe neighborhood that's close to resources, such as grocery shopping and healthcare services. We don't want to move too far away from the "kids," so we can stay connected and be a part of our grandchildren's lives.

Choices I'm facing in this moment:
1) Do we want to have one last family vacation before we sell the cottage?
2) Do we want to buy or rent?
3) Do we want to move to a less expensive neighborhood or stay in the beautiful area we live in now?
4) How much space do we really need?

Which options best support my overall objective?

1) Yes, let's have one last family vacation at the cottage.

2) By selling the big house and the cottage, we can afford to buy a smaller house or condominium and pay cash, so we'd have no mortgage.

3) We love our neighborhood and the friends we have here, so we want to stay in the area.

4) If we stay near the kids, we don't need many guest rooms. A small 2- or 3-bedroom home would be perfect.

Appendix I: Miscellaneous Tools for Choice

∾ Do a Pros and Cons list for each option.

∾ Toss a coin. Whichever way it comes up, are you happy or disappointed? What are you feeling in your body?

∾ Put together a brainstorming group and toss around different options. Having multiple perspectives will help broaden your view, and other people will see options that you hadn't thought of, or ones that you've avoided because they seem frightening or overwhelming to you.

∾ If a choice feels too big for you, how can you either scale it down or break it into doable baby steps?

∾ Take each option and live with it for a day or a week, as if you had chosen that option. How does it feel? What do you notice in your body? What outcome is this mostly likely leading to? What obstacles are in your way? Are they manageable or avoidable? Write down your observations. Do that for each option, then compare your notes. (See also appendix B.)

Appendix J: Suggested Reading

Covey, Stephen R. *The 7 Habits of Highly Effective People: Powerful Lessons in Personal Change.* New York: Simon & Schuster, 2013.

Cross, Wilbur. *Choices With Clout: How to Make Things Happen By Making the Right Decisions Every Day of Your Life.* Lincoln, NE: iUniverse, 2002.

Hammond, John S., Ralph L. Keeney and Howard Raiffa. *Smart Choices: A Practical Guide to Making Better Decisions.* Boston: Harvard Business Reveiw Press, 1999.

McKey, Zoe. *The Critical Mind: Make Better Decisions, Improve Your Judgment, and Think a Step Ahead of Others.* Independently published, 2017.

Schwartz, Barry. T*he Paradox of Choice: Why More Is Less.* New York: HarperCollins, 2009.

Shoukry, A. I. *In or Out: A Practical Guide to Decision-Making.* Independently published, 2017.

Sinetar, Marsha. *Elegant Choices, Healing Choices.* Mahwah, NJ: Paulist Press, 1989.

Taylor, Madison. *The Art of Decision Making: How to Make Better Choices in Love, Life, and Work.* Jersey City, NJ: Make Profits Easy LLC, 2016.

Acknowledgments

Writing a book is never a solo effort. This book started with a teleclass when I was just beginning as a Life Coach. So, I must begin by thanking those who sponsored, co-led and attended those teleclasses, although their names no longer reside in my memory.

Next, of course, my friend and editor, Shanna Richman. I always enjoy our spirited conversations that challenge my thinking and offer me new perspectives on my ideas and opinions.

No person exists in a vacuum, so heart-felt thanks go to all of my friends and family who support and encourage my wild journeys and creative ideas.

And a special thanks to my immediate family: My sister Bonnie, who supports me through challenging times and just makes life better for me, and my mother, Selma, who at 96 doesn't really get what I do anymore, but who showers me with love whenever I see her.

My wish is that everyone who reads this book sees their life get better as a result of it.

About the Author

Sharon Good, BCC, ACC, CLC, is president of Good Life Coaching Inc., and a veteran Life, Career, Retirement and Creativity Coach based in the heart of New York City. She coaches artists to achieve their creative and professional goals and helps individuals from all walks of life create fulfilling lives, unique career paths and enriching retirements.

Sharon has been blessed to share her experience as a Coach, along with decades of personal growth studies, as a coaching instructor for the Life Purpose Institute, the Creativity Coaching Association and New York University's School of Professional Studies, as well as offering personal and professional growth classes at the 92nd Street Y.

Standing on the shoulders of her experience as co-publisher of Excalibur Publishing, Sharon continues to share her written and recorded work through Good Life Press. Her publications include *Creative Marketing Tools for Coaches* and *The Tortoise Workbook: Strategies for Getting Ahead at Your Own Pace*.

Sharon's professional credentials include a BA in Drama and Music from Hofstra University; a certificate in Adult Career Planning and Development from New York University; certification in Life, Life Purpose and Career Coaching from the Life Purpose Institute; and certification in Retirement Coaching from Retirement Options. She is a Board Certified Coach with the Center for Credentialing & Education and an Associate Certified Coach with the International Coach Federation.

Sharon can be contacted via her websites: www.goodlifecoaching.com and www.goodlifepress.com.

CPSIA information can be obtained
at www.ICGtesting.com
Printed in the USA
LVHW090119140519
617744LV00002B/280/P